The *New* Parrot Training Handbook

Revised, Expanded and

Updated with an all new

chapter on speech training.

By Jennifer Hubbard

Book design by Debbie Silverman
Photography by Norman Plate
Illustrations by Kara Hubbard

The New Parrot Training Handbook

Jennifer Hubbard

First Edition Published 1990
The New Parrot Training Handbook Published 1997

The author has made a rigorous attempt to exhaustively research and clarify all advice offered herein, no liability will be assumed due to omissions, inaccuracies, or misinterpretation.

Hubbard, Jennifer
The New Parrot Training Handbook
Parrot Press
1. Parrot Training - Behavior, Intelligence of
Hubbard, Jennifer II. Title

Library of Congress Catalogue Card Number: 96-092980

ISBN 0-9626724-2-4

Printed and bound in the United States.

TABLE OF CONTENTS

TABLE OF CONTENTS

Introduction to the Second Edition

In 1989 I wrote the first edition of The Parrot Training Handbook out of a need that I perceived for a clear, well-organized book on the subject of bird training. As a writer I was disappointed with the books I found on the subject. Though I am not a professional bird trainer, I have trained horses and dogs professionally and I have successfully tamed and trained my own pet parrots. Since 1989 I have streamlined some of my training methods and learned some clever "tricks" for dealing with parrot misbehavior. I have included my new-found knowledge in this edition of the Handbook.

During the years that I have worked with animals, I have seen many very accomplished trainers who have difficulty teaching the training process. These people are expert trainers who achieve excellent results. The problem is that they have so internalized the training process, they forget to explain the individual steps involved. They have completely lost the perspective of the beginner.

Approaching bird training with a beginner's mind and armed with the conviction that I would be successful (based on my previous experience with other animals), I carefully observed the steps that I took. With patience and many mistakes, I discovered and recorded methods for training and taming birds that anyone can employ successfully. This book is the product of trial and error, extensive research, and experience.

I wrote this book as I struggled to understand and train my own birds. I have learned a great deal in this process, and my curiosity has been fueled by it. My goal is to help parrot owners understand their pets more clearly, so that they can live with them more happily. I hope it is clear, simple, and fun to use.

How to Use this Book

This book is laid out so that a beginning trainer with a phobic, mistrustful bird can successfully tame and train their bird. Scan each section and determine where your bird is in the taming and training process. Make sure that your bird is ready to progress to the next level of training before attempting it. Training is a series of carefully calculated steps that, if taken in sequence, are much easier and more effective.

This book is designed to be used like a cookbook or instruction manual. Keep the book handy you while you train your parrot, so that if you get confused or forget a step, you can stop and reread the text.

The print in this book is larger than most books so that people who wear reading glasses may not have to wear them during their training sessions. I have yet to meet a parrot that will leave my glasses on my face.

Each trick has a similar layout. The following page shows what each trick looks like and how the information should be used.

Trick Title

Needs: A list of what you'll need to prepare before beginning the training session.

Training time: This is intended to give you an idea of how long the average bird will be attentive at a particular level of training. It also limits the amount of time you should spend on certain behaviors that are stressful to the parrot.

Description: This section will give a description of the trick and any special goals you'll want to keep in mind.

---

1 Each step in the trick is clearly separated from the next. You must learn to pace your bird and have it master each step before going on to the next one. It will be clear when the bird understands one step of the trick, and quickly responds with the desired behavior. It is not unusual for a bird to master only one step per session. Don't rush training.

---

2 You can expect to train your bird its first complete trick within your first seven sessions.

Notes to the Novice Trainer

Training does not consist of "controlling" a bird's behavior, it is communication in a structured relationship with an animal. This is both a very fine line and a very important one. I don't want to give the impression that animals never need to be controlled. However, I strongly believe that communicating with an animal instead of controlling it will result in a happier, healthier, more trainable animal.

Whether you plan to train your bird to make it a movie star, a neighborhood attraction, or just a happier, more enjoyable pet, training done properly will improve your relationship with your bird.

Training is Communication

I remember, when I was first learning to train animals, how miserable my attempts to produce the desired behaviors were. I have worked with young people and adults, teaching them to train animals, and it is always frustrating for them at first. But as a person begins to give an animal credit for its intellect and emotions, genuine communication between the animal and trainer occurs. This communication greatly increases the success of training.

I imagine the animal's experience of training to be like having someone drive up alongside you on the freeway and point at your back tire. It is nerve wracking trying to figure out what could possibly be wrong as you try to make sense of a complete stranger's hand signals. I picture myself as the wildly gesticulating motorist trying to get through to an animal as we begin our training relationship. I keep this image in mind, to aid me in maintaining patience and empathy with an animal throughout the early sessions.

Training is Paying Attention

The finest animal trainers I have known all have had a few traits in common: they care about their animals, they are consistent and patient, and they concentrate on what they are doing. Because all of these traits are important to successful animal training, I would like to elaborate on each of them.

CARING for an animal means concern for its emotions, well being, and respect for its individuality. It means not forcing an animal to perform behaviors that are beyond its trust level, and not allowing the animal to become willful and headstrong. Just like parenting— firm but caring.

CONSISTENCY means careful thought about a training session before it begins. Decide on the cues and bridges (more on this later) you will use before beginning the session. Don't reward your parrot for an incorrect behavior, and do not reward your parrot for a behavior when it wasn't given the cue to perform it. Patience means appreciating what little progress you will make with certain birds. Patience means keeping training sessions short at first and never abusing your bird's attention span. Patience means keeping your temper with a bird who is willful. And by the way, some birds will not or cannot be trained, but these are the exceptions.

CONCENTRATION means watching your bird attentively and rewarding the small steps it takes towards performing the behavior you want. Rewards must be immediate, so that a connection between the behavior and reward can be established in the parrot's mind.

Concentration means that your body language, voice, and behavior are consistent with what you want the bird to do. I find that a good way to keep my concentration on the training session is to picture the animal performing the behavior we are working on in my mind. In this way, I keep my attention on the task at hand more efficiently. There are some who believe that animals "see" these mental pictures. I don't know if this is true, I personally feel that body language has more to do with it, but visualizing while training is remarkably effective.

Fremont, California
November, 1996

TAMING & TRUST BUILDING

Allow a new pet to acclimate to its new home for at least a month before beginning taming or training. Training can be very stressful.

Taming & Trust Building

If you are considering buying a wild or traumatized bird as a pet because you don't want to spend the money on a hand fed bird, I would strongly encourage you to take the time saving your money for the hand reared baby. If everything goes perfectly (and it almost never does), it will take months to tame a wild or phobic bird, and you may not get much satisfaction from your pet until it is tame.

When this book was first published in 1990 wild caught birds were as common as hand fed birds. Recent restrictions on importation have made it so that wild-caught birds are not very common today. This has been a boon to pet bird lovers since domestically bred, hand raised birds are much better candidates for pets. Birds who are frightened of people and do not accept handling still unfortunately exist. But fortunately many of them can learn to trust humans and will adjust beautifully to a life in human care, given proper guidance. It is my observation that most parrots will bond and form trusting relationships with people if given the right type of attention and guidance. This chapter will guide you thorough some simple methods for gaining you bird's trust.

Taming is the first step in training. The taming process you will use depends on the type of bird you have. If you own a bird with phobic, mistrusting behavior, the taming process will be much more demanding than if your bird is comfortable being handled.

If your bird is new to your home keep handling to a reasonable amount of time at first because the bird needs to learn to play by itself and find its food and water bowls. Birds are fascinating but it is important not to pay too much attention to the bird in the beginning. New bird owners commonly create problems by constantly playing with their new bird at first, and when the novelty wears off, or real life intrudes, the young bird is unprepared to spend time by itself.

Protect the trusting nature of your bird by showing people, especially children, how to handle it properly. A parrot is rarely a good pet for a child. Until children demonstrate real concern for a bird's needs, they should only be allowed supervised time with the bird.

Building Trust & Confidence

Taming a bird is a relatively simple process but it requires patience and sensitivity. The most important skill involved in taming is compassion. Compassion not just for the bird you are working with, but also for your own limitations. If you have attempted to tame a bird unsuccessfully, you either tried to do too much too soon, or you were dealing with a bird that was not willing to become tame. Most failures are attributable to one or both of these factors. This method will shield you from overstepping your limitations, and at the same time, allows for progressive taming. This is not quick, it involves building a trusting relationship, and this takes time. Confidence and trust can quickly be destroyed by impatience and mishandling.

The following methods have several goals:

1. Developing the deepest level of trust possible with the bird. What you probably think of as a "tame" bird is simply a bird that feels safe and trusts its handlers.

2. Forming a dominant and caring relationship with the bird. In human terms I would compare this goal to becoming the bird's firm, caring parent. In my experience a submissive bird is gentler, more playful, less dangerous, and seemingly happier. The only other positive relationship with a bird is as its surrogate mate, and this type of relationship is much too dangerous to condone because the bird will be hostile to everyone but you, and sometimes it will also be hostile to you. As the "parent," you are the caretaker and provider.

What to expect

The process of a bird becoming tame is as individual as birds are themselves. I view it as a growing level of trust and the bird seeking to fill its strong social needs in its new "human flock". The first sign of success is the bird regarding you with interest, perhaps moving toward you and taking food from your hand, and/or attempting to communicate verbally with you.

Be patient, go slowly. Take each part of the taming process one step at a time. Forget your expectations, your bird will trust you when it is ready to, not when you *think* it should. Be patient, be consistent, and keep in mind that you and the bird can live the rest of your lives very happily together, if you take the time now to build a trusting relationship.

Special Considerations

1. WATCH THOSE HANDS, BUDDY!

Hands are very intimidating, and seen as dangerous by most traumatized birds. Even tame, well-adjusted bird are normally nervous around a new person's hands. When working around untame birds, be very conscious of your hands. When you must reach towards a bird, speak softly and move slowly, turning your hands over, in a non-threatening manner.

2. KNOW YOUR LIMITATIONS. I strongly

caution you against forcing physical contact with a bird as a taming method. There are many techniques involving toweling and other forms of restraints that, if done expertly and calmly, can produce results. BUT... if you are taming a bird for the first time, getting the bird restrained will probably be difficult and you and the bird will both be traumatized by the experience.

Although taming is a long, and sometimes boring process, it can be very rewarding for both the bird and the trainer. Keep interaction with a new, traumatized bird

to a minimum for the first few weeks, and then place
its cage where you can talk to it occasionally. If you
delay handling the bird for a month or more, the bird
has already developed some curiosity, and the taming
process progresses more quickly.

Taming a Severely Phobic Bird

Week One

Take the bird to an experienced Avian
Veterinarian to insure that it is healthy.
It is quite likely that the bird has some low
grade bacterial infections and vitamin defi-
ciencies. It is important to insure the bird is
healthy before beginning taming which can
be quite stressful for the bird in the
beginning.

Keep the bird's diet the same as it has
been, perhaps adding a fresh vegetable or
fruit to another dish. Leave the bird alone
as much as possible except for cage clean-
ing this first week.

Week Two

Begin a time limit feeding schedule. Start
creating a positive association through time

limited feeding. This means giving the bird several meals throughout the day. You can feed 3 to 6 times per day, according to your schedule. The goal is to allow the bird to develop some hunger between the times that food is available. You will have to experiment with the proper amounts. Each time you arrive with food, your bird will be relieved of its hunger and the beginning of a positive association with you can take place.

Note: If your schedule does not allow you to offer time limit feeding, leave a pelleted diet in the cage, available to the bird at all times and offer supplemental favorite foods in the same manner as time limit feeding.

Time limit feeding allows you to quickly see what your bird's favorite foods are, after 2-3 weeks you can attempt to lure the bird to eat from your hand with these foods before the food bowls are placed in the cage. If the bird will not take food from your hand, try again in 2 weeks. Spending time with the bird while it consumes its favorite foods is another way to build a positive association in the bird's mind.

Tip: It is sometimes easier to convert a bird from a seed based diet to a balanced manufactured/pelleted diet with time limit feeding.

Weeks 3 & 4

Spend two short periods each day talking with the bird. This is a little easier if the bird is vocalizing. If the bird is making noises, repeat them while the bird can see you, if the bird answers, improvise the sound a little. If the bird does not answer, try "talking" from another room. If the bird is not vocalizing, some of the most successful noises to stimulate vocalization are a soft "clucking" made with your tongue or higher pitched, soft, lilting sounds.

Be patient. Allow the bird to get used to you and keep handling to a minimum for the first 2 - 4 months, or until the bird shows strong signs of curiosity towards you and is readily accepting food from your hand. Although this seems like a long time, my experience has been more positive when I delay extensive physical contact with a bird for some time. I have had fewer problems and more dramatic results with a bird that is familiar with me, and has grown to trust me enough to give me the benefit of the doubt when the inevitable stressful situation arises while we are together.

Weeks 4 through 16/18

Increase interaction. Gradually increase your interaction with the bird during this time. Place the bird's cage in a place where you spend a lot of time, quietly. i.e.: near the television, in your study, in your workshop (although beware of noxious fumes). You are playing on the bird's need for social interaction, and you are allowing the bird to get to know you and trust that you are not going to harm it.

Continue Verbal Interaction. Imitate the noises that your bird makes. Over time, I've discovered that this is the most effective way of building a relationship with a traumatized bird. With a silent bird you will hear the first noises when you are in another room or have been ignoring the bird for a while. The bird is essentially calling for its flock, you should respond in a tone as close to the one the bird is making as possible. Answering its call is a form of communication that can evolve into its own language. This behavior is very natural for birds in the wild where they have been observed speaking a "flock specific" language with distinct variations used only with their mates.

The parrots I have had the most success with have participated in this language development by repeating words and phrases I say, but this seems to be secondary to my repeating their noises.

Teaching a bird to trust your hands.

The purpose of this exercise is to teach the bird that you won't "force" it with your hands. As a bird learns that your hands are gentle and can offer some physical contact (which many of the phobic birds I have encountered are desperately in need of) it will be much easier and safer to teach it to perch quietly on your hand.

Keep your hands relaxed and stop any motion towards your bird if it becomes defensive.

1 Rest your hands near the bird, continue to talk to the bird. This should be a very calm, quiet exercise. If the bird growls or flees, you are trying to progress too quickly.

2 As the bird relaxes around your hands make your first contact. Gently stroke your bird's foot or leg with your finger, allow the bird to nudge you with its beak, remain relaxed, if the bird objects move your hand beside its foot and stop. If the bird tries to grab your finger in its beak, relax and allow the bird to gently explore your finger. As long as you and the bird are relaxed it is highly unlikely that the bird will bite. Just remember to keep your fingers relaxed.

During this exercise you can "force" yourself to relax by taking long, slow, deep breaths, while you think about filling your belly with air.

3 If the bird is relaxed while being touched, begin gently picking up its toes and massage the toe gently.

Once the bird is allowing you to gently hold its toes, you are ready to progress to hand training.

More Trust Building Methods
for somewhat phobic birds

It isn't necessary to use all of these steps with every bird. As soon as your bird is anxious to be with you, confidently hopping onto your hand, and/or comfortably looking you in the eye, you are ready to begin training.

Trust is the foundation on which any training regimen should be built. When training a parrot, first spend time building the parrot's confidence in you. Once you have a parrot's trust, getting their attention is much simpler. Birds are social animals who will be anxious for whatever time and contact they can have with their trusted friends. Birds get lonely and display psychic disorders like feather plucking if they do not have a close, trusting relationship.

Trust-building can be done in many ways. On the following pages you'll find a few methods to use with tame birds to get them ready for training.

When working with a new bird, clasp your hands behind your back. Try this with the next unfamiliar bird you meet, use only eye contact, smile and speak in a soft, upbeat voice.

ONE

Sit quietly with your bird.

When you have 15-30 minutes to spend with your bird, sit down with it in a relatively quiet place (in front of the TV is O.K. for most birds). Start with scratching and ruffling the feathers at the back of its head. After a few minutes of this, some parrots will allow you to scratch anywhere on their body. Take it slowly, move from the head to the top of the neck, speaking softly to the parrot.

The bird may have to go through some trust building exercises with each member of the family who wants to handle it.

Do not try to force a bird to allow more contact than it is comfortable with-coax it to let you scratch under its wings, its legs, stroke its feet, etc. An essential element to gaining a bird's trust is letting the bird dictate how much, how soon. Most birds will forget they were ever squeamish about letting you handle them. This exercise also makes wing and nail clipping a breeze

TWO

Share food or spoon feed.

Warm healthy foods may be greedily consumed. Let the bird have their fill as long as the food is not full of sugar, salt or fat. Most birds enjoy having a taste of whatever you are eating, and may put their trust in a person who feeds them. Spoon feeding will have the same affect on some birds as hand-feeding. Spoon feeding can be done with anything you both enjoy. Maintain eye contact (but don't stare down a shy bird) and speak softly to the bird while feeding it.

> Talk to your bird in the most soothing voice possible, and do not raise your voice. If you have a good singing voice, lullabies are a wonderful method for calming birds.

THREE

Get someone else to do your dirty work.

So that the bird does not associate you with fear and pain, have someone else handle unpleasant tasks like nail and wing clipping.

FOUR

Imitate the bird's gestures and sounds.

This can be a particularly useful method if the bird calls to you when you leave the room. Imitation is used by most wild animal trainers, to gain an animal's trust. If the bird is ignoring you, shutting its eyes, or looking away as soon as you make eye contact, it is shy and afraid. Make a game out of this behavior by slowly shutting your eyes or turning your head. Let the bird be the one looking at you. This is a marvelous game for increasing a bird's confidence.

Anthropologists speed up the process of trust-building through the use of imitation. Watch your bird, being careful not to stare (this is aggressive behavior), and imitate its behavior.

FIVE

Rescue the bird from a threatening situation.

If your bird somehow gets into trouble, calmly get it out of harm's way. This method will not be useful unless you can calmly accept the possibility of getting bitten. A scared bird is unpredictable, if this frightens you, don't rescue your bird without a towel to place over its head.

SIX

Lure the bird to you.

Clasp your hands behind your back and allow your eyes and voice to communicate how much you like the bird. Smile, tell the bird how beautiful it is using an upbeat (but not excited) tone of voice. Birds are very visual and often respond to a happy, interested person, who does not invade their personal space by "inviting" the person to come to them. If the bird leans toward you or offers you its foot, slowly move towards the bird and let it hold your finger in its foot or gently scratch its head. It is important in this exercise to let the bird make the first move.

SEVEN

Sing, hum or whistle.

Birds can respond dramatically to music. I usually try lullabies with some dramatic results. If you can't carry a tune, listen to some soothing music and hum along. If you want to have a little fun try some fast-paced music and see how it influences your bird's mood. Take care when handling a bird that is wound up from high energy music, though, some birds can get quite rowdy!

TALKING & SPEECH TRAINING

*Besides being fun and enter-
taining, parrot speech is also
fascinating. Research is showing
that parrots do much more than
simply mimic sounds, that they
are on some level, attempting
to communicate with us.*

A talking bird is a wonderful, whimsical thing. At times, I convince myself that since I love my birds with equal intensity whether they talk or not, that talking is not that important. Well, of course it isn't everything, but it's one of the delightful things that pet birds can do. Each time one of my birds talks, sings or makes a joyful, happy series of noises, I stop, and laugh . . . and wonder.

How Parrot Vocalization is Unique

Many different types of birds use vocalizations for communication and identification of their flocks, but parrots stand alone in their use of vocalizations in some remarkable ways.

One example of this is the research done with many different types of songbirds showing that there is a narrow window in the songbird's youth in which it can learn its flock's song. It is clear that parrots retain the ability to learn "new songs" for their entire lifetime, I have personally witnessed several wild-caught adult parrots (ages were estimated at 5+ years based on the beak size and condition of the feet) learn their first English words, and I have met quite a few parrots in their teens and twenties who were constantly increasing their vocabulary. This in itself indicates a more advanced intelligence and learning process for the parrot as opposed to other types of birds whose song or vocalizations have been analyzed.

"Parroting" is Inaccurate

Ongoing research shows that parrots have the ability to associate words with objects. This is referred to as labeling. Not only have the research parrots recognized and identified objects by name, they have also exhibited awareness of "object permanence". This means that they understand that things still exist when they cannot see them. The concept of object permanence had been considered to be beyond the range of animal intelligence.

Most baffling to me though, is the demonstrated ability of parrots to understand syntax and form sentences. Several anecdotes of parrots that would greet single individuals and groups with the proper singular and plural forms (i.e., "Hi guys" and "Hi guy") are reported in many popular magazines. One anecdote is told about a German parrot who would do this reliably, and the German singular and plural form of greeting are remarkably different.

There is no guarantee that a particular bird will choose to communicate verbally, or even play with sounds. But an understanding of the capacity of parrots to use and understand language is an important basis for a discussion on speech training methods. My methods are devised from conversations with hundreds of bird owners, several other bird behaviorists, the tentative scientific evidence that exists today, and my own personal experience.

It would seem that the way that birds are taught to speak is the way that they will speak. For instance, repetitive records and tapes are efficient ways to teach your bird to speak, sing or whistle, but they will not produce intelligent speech patterns. I am not condemning or criticizing these methods, but their limitations should be understood before they are used.

Actually, I do want to add a little personal criticism of repetitive training methods like records and tapes. I once rescued a bird who was taught to speak with this method. Whenever she wanted something she would repeat "Pretty Boy!", over and over and over. After four years into our life together this got really old. On the other hand, the owner who taught her this said an enthusiastic "Yeah!" whenever she repeated a phrase. She also picked up this "Yeah!" and it was always used appropriately when the bird was very pleased with something like a bath or favorite food, this vocalization was always delightful and touching. So I don't highly recommend speech training records, except perhaps to teach a specific song like, Happy Birthday.

Now, without further ado, here are several methods for training birds to speak.

Method One — Repetition

By using a repetitive loop tape, available at most record stores and stores that sell answering machines, you can record a word, song, or phrase and play it repeatedly for your bird. If you make your own recording use an animated, upbeat or emotionally-charged tone of voice. Birds respond to the energy level behind words.

Regular sessions, for an hour or less, once or twice a day are usually effective. It is not a good idea to play something constantly to your bird, since they will probably adjust to it and tune it out.

Obviously, you can also use this method by repeating a word or phrase to the bird yourself. Compact discs and pre-recorded cassettes made specifically for teaching birds to speak are available.

Outcome: The bird will repeat the song, phrase or word, usually when cued with the word or the beginning of the phrase or song. Caution: Some birds will repeat the phrases they learn endlessly.

Method Two — Context Speech

This method of teaching birds to speak takes more time but less concentrated effort.

Decide on a few words that you can use in context, such as, "Hi, Bye, Good Morning, Good Night, See you later." Use the words frequently around your bird and say them in context.

Allow the bird time to pick up new words. Certain words may catch the bird's fancy and be repeated quickly while others take time or never become a part of the bird's vocabulary.

If you are successful with this method, advance to teaching the bird the names of things. Examples are: pointing out animals or interesting objects and saying their names, saying the name of a favorite food while offering it to the bird, or pointing to a favorite family member and saying their name.

Method Three — One of the Family

This method involves a lifestyle change for you and your bird. It seems remarkably simple, but for some of us involves bringing a bird, which has been relegated to a special room or corner, into the center of family life.

Include the bird into family activities, especially where the family congregates for meals, television, conversation or games. Birds who live in the hubbub of homes seem to become a part of the family/flock, and use speech as a way to get attention and communicate.

I have observed that birds who are included in family life by placing their cages in the TV room, living room, or most active room in the house are most likely to be birds who talk.

Placing a pet bird in the family's main living space where it can be a part of the family is a good idea for your bird's emotional well-being too!

Outcome: Spontaneous speech. Probably the most enjoyable type of parrot speech because the bird's own unique personality and view of the world emerges.

Method Four — The Model/Rival Technique

If you have a partner to help you train your bird, and you are not afraid of some work, the method being used by Dr. Irene Pepperberg with her studies of language in African Greys is a wonderful thing to try. This method is called the Model/Rival Technique. The method was developed in the 1950's by German scientist Dietmar Todt to train parrots to answer questions in a laboratory setting. In this method, two people must be available and willing to work consistently with the bird.

An important aspect of Model/Rival Technique is the reward. Parrots are social animals (to differing degrees) and interaction is one reward, but parrots also respond to rewards of food and objects to explore.

Some research suggests that parrots are capable of mimicking any sound that they hear within the first year (or so) of their life.

You may have noticed that a reward has not been mentioned in any of the other techniques I describe. There are two reasons for this. The first is that a bird that learns to speak for a reward will talk whenever it sees someone with food in their hand. The second reason is the lack of meaning inherent in the reward.

If, for instance, you reward a parrot with a nut for saying, "How are you?" you are forming a pattern in the parrots brain that "How are you?" is just one more way of saying, "give me a nut." If however you reward the bird with attention and animated talk, then the bird will learn that "How are you?" is a way of interacting with you. Additionally, the phrase "How are you?" is not appropriate for model/rival technique. Choose sentences or words that name objects that the parrot enjoys. Examples are foods and small safe objects like keys, corks and small hand toys.

In model/rival the parrot is viewed as a part of a triad. Two human beings model the behavior that is desired from the parrot.

Example: Training a Parrot the Label "Nut"

In this example the two humans will attempt to train the parrot to ask for a nut by name.

Standing in front of the parrot, both trainers should be able to establish eye contact with one another or the parrot. Trainer #1 begins.

Trainer #1: Holds up a nut for the parrot and other human to see. Trainer #1 says, "Nut".

Trainer #2: Looks interested, looks at parrot, looks back at trainer #1, and says, "Nut"

Trainer #1: Gives trainer #2 the nut and praises and pays attention to trainer #2.

This is repeated several times, and then trainer #1 and #2 switch roles. The parrot is always addressed in the same manner as the other trainer. When the parrot says, "Nut", the bird receives the nut and gets the attention and praise of both trainers.

Outcome: Dr. Pepperberg's research strongly suggests that parrots have the capacity to understand what they are asking for.

> Note: I direct readers interested in learning more about Dr. Irene Pepperberg's studies of bird communication and intelligence to an article in the September 1991 issue of Audubon magazine about her work.

In Conclusion

A friend of mine was birdsitting for a friend. The parrot had never spoken and my friend thought it would be a nice surprise to teach the bird to say Hello. She stood by the cage and repeated the word over and over, day after day, while the bird remained silent.

One day as she was standing by the cage patiently repeating the word "Hello" to the bird, the family dog who had been watching all along looked up at her and said, "Hello!" She decided to give up on the bird.

This bird was a species with a reputation for talking, my friend has a high pitched voice which parrots seem fond of mimicking, she is an energetic happy person. All of these things seem to be positive indicators of a bird that will talk but this one never did. I don't know why.

I hope that you will embark on a speech training project with the goal of learning more about your bird, and not with any other specific goal in mind. The outcome you have will depend on the complex relationship that you and your bird share and your bird's own physiology and personality.

INTRODUCTION TO TRAINING

A well-trained parrot is one of the most entertaining pets a person can live with. Once a parrot has learned new ways to get attention it may become a ham. I have watched trick-trained parrots desperately going through their entire repertoire of tricks again and again to get the attention of a group of people who were watching another bird go through its paces.

Preparation

You must take several preliminary steps before you begin to trick-train your parrot. Unless you properly prepare yourself and your bird for trick-training, your results will be mixed.

A quiet place: Set up your training headquarters where you'll have the least distractions—if possible, choose a room that can be closed off for the entire session. Working in a room where the parrot cannot see its cage is the best idea. Don't forget, your jewelry and watch are a distraction. Remove them.

The perch: A T-stand or simple perch is the best way to keep your parrot's attention focused on the training session. If you do not already own a T-stand, the back of a chair can be used as long as the bird can grip the chair back comfortably. Do not have toys or dishes on the training perch that can distract the bird.

Treat acclimation: The training reward must be a small size that can be swallowed quickly. I use shelled peanuts, (broken in half), shelled sunflower seeds, or pieces of fruit for overweight birds.

If your parrot does not already have a favorite treat, you can acclimate it by adding 1-2 tablespoons of the intended treat to its food for approximately two weeks. Begin to watch for signs that it has eaten the special treat first. Now comes the nasty part; eliminate the treat from its diet. Only offer this food during training sessions. When a treat acclimated bird, who knows a few tricks, sees its treats, they will usually do one of their tricks to try to get one.

If your parrot does not seem interested in the treat or the training sessions, it can help to remove all food from its cage for 1-3 hours before the training session. Experiment with the amount of time it takes to peak your own bird's appetite.

> Note: Sunflower seeds have a great deal of oil in them, this means two things: they are fattening (so are peanuts) and they spoil quickly. I buy shelled, unsalted sunflower seeds from a health food store; human, food-grade seeds are much less likely to have sat in storage, and will cause less digestive problems for your bird.

Bridging: A bridge is a sound cue that lets your bird know it has done what you wanted and is about to get a reward. The use of a bridge is essential in getting your bird to associate the reward with its behavior. Training without a bridge is considerably slower than otherwise.

Clickers and other Bridges: Many animal trainers make use of clickers as a bridge. I have seen them used, and think they are wonderful, but I prefer to train my birds with one hand free (One hand is at the ready with a treat, at all times).

I prefer to use a verbal bridge, not only because I naturally respond with an immediate "good," when my birds behave, but also because I have a tendency to misplace little things like clickers. I use "Good!" in an enthusiastic, pleasant tone. You can choose any phrase you like, keeping in mind that your bird may learn to repeat it. The most important criteria for choosing a successful bridge is that the word comes naturally to you. Your bridge does not have to be a word, any short, distinct, sound will do.

Cues: A wonderful thing about parrot training is that some birds will not only perform the desired behavior but they will also repeat the verbal cue. I always take this possibility into consideration when deciding what cue I will use.

If you are training your bird with the hope of getting it to perform professionally, always progress to the use of non-verbal hand cues in the later stages of training.

Discipline: Unlike some other animals, birds do not understand physical discipline. Birds are rarely aggressive in the wild—the act of fluffing up their feathers (called "showing" or "displaying") is about as aggressive as they get*. Striking, hitting, shouting at, or otherwise responding violently to a bird will not produce

* With the notable exception of some male birds in captive breeding situations who have been known to kill or seriously injure their mates.

desirable results. I strongly advise you not to strike a bird at any time, it confuses them, does not achieve anything positive in curbing or changing their behavior and causes them to lose faith in you.

However, there are ways to discipline birds. Social isolation is undesirable and can be the bird equivalent of a "time out". Restricted movement can work wonders on some biting behavior and the Parrot Hold (see page 63) technique is well worth the time it will take you to learn it. If you are quick, you can attempt to restrain a bird from biting or other undesired behaviors while saying "BAD" or "NO". If an undesirable outcome occurs for the bird, like isolation or restricted movement, the bird will begin to understand the general meaning of "NO" or "BAD". Consistency is the key.

Empathy is one of the most important tools that you'll use in taming and training your parrot.

The most important consideration in choosing a discipline for your bird, is that it suits the bird's personality. An effective discipline for a wild-caught bird is being placed on the floor, where it will feel insecure. For a hand-raised baby this will not work and the worst fate is usually isolation. Individual birds are different. You may already know the best discipline for your bird as long as it's not frightening for the bird, use it.

Note: When using your voice to convey displeasure, have a friend listen to see if your voice is too loud, or threatening. Don't shout.

DISCIPLINE IS NOT THE KEY

To create a peaceful and fulfilling relationship with a bird, it is important that the bird sees you as the dominant member in the relationship. Dominance is not a brutal display of power, it is a calm insistence of setting the rules of your life together. As you work through the techniques in this book, you will be demonstrating to your bird that you are trustworthy and sensitive to its needs, but not a pushover. Discipline is simply a way of letting your bird know that its current behavior is unacceptable, it will not form the basis of a strong and happy relationship with your pet, it is just a communication about certain behavior.

Think like a parrot...

Empathy is one of the most important tools that you'll use in taming and training your parrot. I believe that birds experience emotions somewhat like our own but this is a tricky thing to understand fully.

Birds, usually do not think before they act, and cannot conceive of the way that their actions affect us physically or emotionally. Your bird cannot experience life the way you do – its senses are different, its understanding of each situation is limited and it is an animal with a strong instinct of being vulnerable to predators. Our birds react based on their level of faith in us and their own personality.

Training can cause some fear, impatience or anger in your bird. It is very important to recognize when your bird has had enough and to slow down, perhaps to back up and return to something non-threatening and enjoyable.

BEHAVIOR CONDITIONING

This section covers behaviors that can be conditioned, such as hand taming and potty training – what I think of as "good citizenship" training which can alleviate some of the most bothersome parts of owning a bird. This section also covers methods for eradicating bad habits common to birds such as biting and screaming. Look over this section and work on behaviors that you want your bird to perform (or not to perform) before beginning trick training.

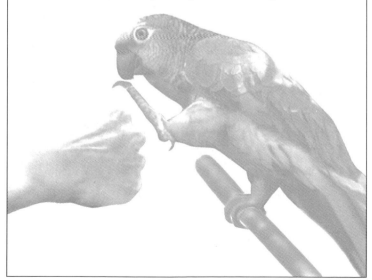

Potty Training

Needs: Newspaper, Trash Can or Litter Tray
The reward is praise and attention
Verbal Cue (sound or word)

Lesson Time: Spend time working on this behavior each day, for at least 30 minutes. This is not a stressful process and the more time you spend, the better your chances for success.

Description: Most people do not realize how easily birds can be potty trained. Every bird can learn some form of potty training. Some become quite responsible for going in the right place without being told constantly, while others will poop "on command". Many birds learn this behavior rapidly others will take more time, but it is well worth your time and effort.

The first step in potty training is to connect a word or gesture (a word is much easier) in the bird's mind to the act of going to the bathroom.

1 While playing with your bird, wait for it to show signs of needing to defecate. Birds will differ in the signs they exhibit, some drop their tail and wiggle back and forth, others stay

still with a fixed stare. Some run around nervously, and I'm sure there are behaviors that I haven't observed. As your bird indicates its need to go, use your cue word or sound until the bird goes to the bathroom. When the bird defecates, praise the bird. Do this casually for a few days.

Caution: *Birds need to defecate about every 20 minutes to stay healthy and they do not have the anatomical structure to hold on indefinitely. Potty Training does not mean that your bird will now be able to hold on for hours at a time, and if you do not pay attention while playing with your bird and give it the opportunity to go to the bathroom, it will do it anyway.*

If you're lucky, your parrot will begin to notify you of its need by saying its cue, so choose something you'll want to hear in mixed company. Several birds I have seen and heard of have developed this behavior.

Note: Uh, Oh! is a cute cue for potty training and it is as inoffensive as can be when company is over.

The second step is to turn the word the bird now associates with defecating into a cue. Once again wait for your bird to indicate the need to defecate and do something to distract it while you take the bird to the receptacle you have decided to use— perhaps a piece of newspaper placed on the floor. Be consistent with the receptacle you use, it is part of the conditioned response.

Choosing an area that the bird can get to on its own may work out very well, too, since I have known several birds that were self-policing about their potty training (now that's a great trick!).

2 Place the bird on, or in, the potty you have provided and cue it to go. Once the parrot evacuates, bridge and reward with praise and attention. Repeat this conditioning at least once a day, more if possible.

The third step is to get the bird to defecate on cue. In order to do this, you need to know about how often your bird needs to defecate (every twenty minutes seems to be standard in mature parrots, more often in birds less than a year old).

3 Just before the time when your bird would defecate on its own, hold it over the potty you have chosen and calmly cue it to go. Be patient, and calmly repeat the cue until the bird defecates. Once the bird defecates, Reward with praise and positive attention. Repeat this lesson at least once a day.

ACCIDENTS DO HAPPEN

Birds instinctively empty their bowels at any sign of danger as a precursor to fleeing. The most well-trained bird will have "accidents" if startled or under emotional stress.

Hand Training

Training your parrot to obediently step onto your hand and calmly sit still is the most important behavior you will teach your parrot.
I have repeatedly seen this single behavior transform my relationship with a bird. It is the cornerstone to establishing yourself as the rule-maker in the relationship, gaining your bird's trust and making life simpler and safer for you and your bird.

LESSON ONE

Needs: No treats, unless absolutely necessary
          Reward with a head scratch
          Cue
          Bridge

 Lesson Time: 5-15 minutes depending on the bird's attention span

Description: Obediently and calmly stepping onto your hand is essential for your bird's safety. I sometimes have to rescue a bird from a dangerous situation (or from soiling

something with droppings), and the ability to put my hand in front of a bird and give it a cue to step on (I use the word "Up") immediately reoriented the bird, and averted a few disasters. I enjoy a chorus of "Up, Up, Up!" when I enter the bird room. I have also seen "Going up!" used, so that it sounds like an elevator operator, it's adorable to see a bird saying this as it is being lifted off of its perch. Unless your bird is highly resistant, don't allow it to expect a reward for this behavior. This behavior is obedience and safety related (i.e., for the birds own good) and should evolve into a conditioned response (as opposed to a trick). I strongly recommend that you try to evoke this behavior without treats first. It's inconvenient to have to carry treats with you every time you want or need to move your bird.

It is important not to start hand taming from within the cage. If you cannot get your bird out, open the cage door and wait until it comes to the door. A bird can be dangerous when it is protecting its "territory".

1 Hold your hand against the bird's chest so that it can step up onto the knuckles of your index finger and the crook of your thumb. Apply slight pressure to coax the bird onto your hand while using your verbal cue.

2 If the bird resists, speak soothingly and keep your hand at the bird's chest with gentle pressure. Say something to calm the bird, such as, "It's O.K., up!" And persist. Allowing a bird to not perform this behavior because of biting is a poor way to begin your training relationship. See the tips for hand training a biter if the bird is really bad,

3 Once the bird is on your hand, gently close your thumb over its feet. The bird will not like it and will attempt to get its foot on top of your thumb, but continue to replace your thumb gently on top of the bird's feet. Teaching a bird to accept your thumb lying over its feet will begin to remind you of thumb wrestling, but be patient. Soon the bird will accept this contact. Later, if you are carrying the bird around and it attempts to fly away, you can restrain the bird for its own safety with a slight pressure from your thumb (place your free hand in front of the bird's chest as it tries to flee to keep it upright).

Hand Training

LESSON TWO

Description: Once your bird is confidently hopping onto
your hand, the second step in hand taming is having the bird
calmly sit on your hand. Many birds will attempt to climb
up to your shoulder or fly off of your hand. A bird needs to
stay on your hand as a simple, and safe, method of trans-
portation. I find it comforting that I can get a sick bird to
sit calmly on my hand for a trip to the vet, rather than
further stressing it by using a carrier, or manhandling it.

Needs: No treats, unless absolutely necessary
Reward with a head scratch
Cue
Bridge

 Lesson Time: 5-15 minutes depending on the bird's attention span

---

1 Once your bird is on your hand, it will probably attempt to climb up your arm. Do not allow the bird to climb up to your shoulder. It must learn to sit calmly on your hand. Use your free hand to block the bird's progress up your arm—and if necessary, let it perch on your free hand.

---

2 Continue replacing the bird on the crook of your hand each time it attempts to climb up your arm. Gently place your thumb over the bird's toes. Each time the bird sits calmly for a few seconds, bridge and reward.

---

3 In this behavior, unlike the others, the bridge remains constant, i.e., "good", while the reward will be removed once the bird has learned how to get onto your hand and sit

---

quietly. A bird can learn this behavior without receiving any reward (other than being out of its cage with you). Attempt to condition this behavior without a reward, but if you feel one is needed, use it.

If you choose to let your bird sit on your shoulder, place it there from your hand, using another verbal cue (e.g., "on the shoulder") while doing so. Letting the bird climb up your arm erases what you have just taught it.

The Next Step

Once your bird has learned this behavior you can comfortably and safely transport it or trick train it anywhere. It is usually simpler to keep a bird's attention when the bird is on a T-stand or simple perch, but let your bird graduate to doing its tricks from your hand so you can take the show on the road.

Now that your parrot has learned the proper way to get onto your hand and sit quietly, be sure that other family members or handlers don't allow the bird to break the rules.

Tips for Hand Training the Biting Bird

The purpose of hand taming is to teach a bird a cue that means "Get up onto my hand" once the bird is there, the trainer also reliably demonstrates to the bird that it is safe to be on their hand.

In the wild a parrot will test the steadiness of a branch with its beak before stepping onto it. Many novices mistake this testing with biting behavior and quickly pull their hand away, leaving the parrot off balance. It only takes one experience like this for a parrot to respond to a proffered hand with a firm nip. Using a cue allows you and the bird to firmly establish what you are asking, and what the bird can expect. It is crucial that the bird can rely on you to keep your hand steady while it steps up and once it is on your hand. This may mean tolerating a bite from a bird testing you without dropping the bird (and it's not much fun). I use the cue "up" and my birds will respond by raising one foot to step up, as soon as I say the word.

When hand taming a biting bird, a small dowel or branch can be used to protect your hand from the bird's beak. Do not use the dowel in a controlling manner, only use it to prevent the bird's beak from reaching your hand. Trying to control instinctual or defensive behavior invariably makes the behavior worse. Understanding and accommodating a bird's fear will allow the bird to come to terms with you in a gentle, trusting way.

SOLVING BEHAVIOR PROBLEMS

In this section I will share some of my methods for dealing with biting and screaming. I have discovered that trust building and hand training will cause many of these problems to disappear. Here are some methods that I have used successfully with a variety of birds.

Understanding Biting Behavior

Personally, biting is my least favorite aspect of bird ownership. A bite from a pet bird feels like a personal rejection. I used to think that a bite felt worse emotionally than physically, as if the bird was trying to let me know that it severely disliked me. Over the years I have learned to understand that my emotional reaction is not well founded.

Improper hand training is the most common cause of biting behavior in birds.

Through experience and research I have come to suspect that biting is not a form of rejection, but of communication. A bite can mean many things, but most commonly your bird is trying to tell you one of the following things;

"you're scaring me",

"you have entered my territory, uninvited",

"I'm tired and grouchy" or,

"I want to be above you in the pecking order".

Let's look at what your biting bird may be trying to tell you and explore some solutions to the problem.

"You're scaring me"

This biting behavior is an instinctive response to fear. There is only one way to curb this biting behavior, by earning the bird's trust and not doing things that frighten it. I have watched many people displaying nervous behavior while advancing their hand towards a bird, the tamest bird will probably bite them. My observation leads me to believe that animals take their cues of how to react from us. Nervous people cause nervous pets. Bites from frightened birds might be accompanied by growling and can be very severe.

WHAT TO DO:

1. Use Trust Building Exercises (pages 18-22)

2. When working with the bird, if you are feeling nervous take slow, deliberate, deep breaths. This will do two things, it will make you appear calm to the bird, and it will diminish your nervousness.

3. Go through the Hand Training Lessons at a relaxed, unhurried pace (pages 48-52)

"You have entered my territory, uninvited"

Moving suddenly into a bird's "personal space" or cage can often result in a vicious bite. This biting is a sign of mistrust. The bird is protecting its territory whether

it's an entire cage or just its own body. As your relationship with the bird develops, this behavior should
disappear. Birds who have been left for too long inside
their cages become neurotically protective of their
cage. It is easiest to move the bird into a new cage and
insure that it gets out often, at a minimum once a day
for an extended period of time.

WHAT TO DO:

1. Use Trust Building Exercises
(pages 18-22)

2. Let the bird invite you into its territory.
When you approach a bird that is
demonstrating territorial displays, this
usually includes tail flaring, rocking from
foot to foot, rapidly contracting and
dilating pupils and/or an open-beaked
threat, stop and place both hands behind
your back. Talk to the bird, let your interest in the bird show on your face. Smile,
talk in a soothing voice until the bird
relaxes. Slowly move closer to the bird.
The bird may begin to lean toward you or
even offer you its foot. You are soliciting
an invitation into the bird's territory. It's
best if the bird wants to interact with you
and this usually takes patience.

3. Go through the Hand Training Lessons
   (pages 48-52)

"I'm tired and grouchy"

Are you receiving most of your bites late in the
evening? Your bird is up past its bedtime! This biting
behavior is the simplest to remedy. Birds need a lot of
sleep each night, depending on the bird this can be
10-14 hours, and you must experiment to find the
ideal amount of sleep your bird needs. Your bird needs
rest in a dark, quiet area. If your bird lives in a central
area of the house (which is a very good idea) where
people are up late watching TV, talking or leaving
lights on, find a dark quiet space that the bird can
have for a "bedroom". You can use a spare room, the
garage, a second bathroom, even a large coat closet.

"I'm above you in the pecking order"

This type of bite is often described as, "the bird bit me
for no reason", these bites come out of nowhere, the
bird is playing, or resting and then runs over to nip (or
nail) someone. It is not uncommon for the bird to
travel out of its way to deliver this type of bite. I
believe that this is an attempt by the bird to establish
its place in its flock (your family). The person receiving these bites needs to make it clear to the bird that
they will not be pushed around.

WHAT TO DO:

1. Have this person go through some trust building exercises, more to build their confidence in working with the parrot (who is obviously not really frightened of this person) than to build the parrot's trust. (Pages 18-22)

2. After hand training the bird, have this person work on enforcing the hand training cue from neutral settings (somewhere unfamiliar to the bird).

3. Once the bird and person have established some trust, the dominance biting may still occur. The best response I have found is the Parrot Hold (as shown at right).

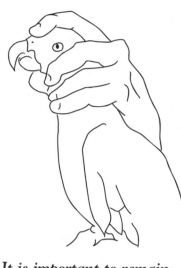

Parrot Hold

You can use the parrot hold to restrain a biting parrot. It calms down most birds and prevents them from biting again

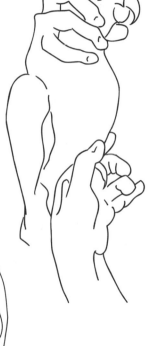

It is important to remain relaxed while doing this. Do not grip tightly. Slowly release the bird when it calms down.

Sometimes a Bite is Not a Bite. . .

In order to cure a biting problem, you must first determine its cause and that will determine the cure. It is also important to understand that there are bite-like behaviors in birds that are not biting. The parrot uses its beak for many of the same things that we use our hands. A parrot will use its beak as a third "claw", in order to climb or catch its balance and to explore unfamiliar objects. A parrot will test a branch it is about to climb onto to make sure it is sturdy, it will often do the same thing with a strangers hand or arm.

The Young Bird and the Beaking Stage

As a bird grows up, it learns about its environment through sight, sound, smell, taste and touch. Birds, go through a stage where everything is explored with their beaks. There is a sensory center on the tip of the parrot's beak, and the "beaking stage" is a period of exploring the world through touch.

During this period (usually before one year of age) some birds develop bad biting habits. In some cases the bird will learn that it can control some people through judicious use of its beak. It is imperative that you begin hand training with a bird exhibiting this behavior as soon as possible. If the biting has already gotten severe, see the tip for hand training a biting bird on page 55.

In some young birds there is a lack of guidance about the amount of pressure that can be exerted on a finger. If you observe a bonded pair of parrots preening one another you can see that they give one another feedback about how the preening feels (this usually takes the form of a squawk and swinging the beak around to the offending preener). So, it is not surprising that any bird can be taught to respect your fingers through feedback. Try the following technique;

While you are spending time with your bird, particularly during a time of day when your bird has a quiet energy level, allow your bird to explore your fingers. Reciprocate by gently stroking or scratching the bird's beak. When the bird exerts even a little too much pressure, respond by "flinching" a little, and saying *ow!* Don't be too dramatic, just disapproving. Allow the bird to explore your fingers again, praise the bird while it is being gentle, and respond immediately when your bird exerts too much pressure.

A bird that does not learn to be gentle with fingers and hands should not be allowed to come into contact with them with its beak.

About Wearing Gloves

Some trainers recommend against wearing gloves to handle a biter. The theory is that it reminds imported birds of their first contact with humans.

If you own a wild-caught bird or a severe biter, you can wash a pair of gloves thoroughly and place them in the cage where the bird can get used to them. You can even place a treat in the palm of one the gloves while it is in the bird's cage. There is no reason to subject yourself to severe biting, and you can acclimate a bird to ignore a pair of gloves.

Once the bird has stopped biting, stop wearing the gloves during handling.

Screaming

Screaming is another annoying habit a pet parrot can acquire. Unfortunately, it is a natural behavior for many parrots—a way of expressing their anger, happiness, and declaring their presence to the world. There are many reasons why birds scream and the way you should respond depends on the root cause.

The: Hello World, I'm a Healthy Happy Parrot!

Morning and evening bouts of screaming are a natural behavior for parrots. These bouts usually coincide with sunrise and sunset and last for a few minutes at most. Many people learn to accept this behavior, and I have found that even my neighbors did not mind it, once I explained what it was. If you are in a situation where you need to curb this behavior, keeping the bird from being aware of sunrise or sunset will usually prevent the morning or evening squawk.

The Cry For Attention

It is an instinct for a parrot to call for its flock or its parents. We humans also respond to this squawking by turning our attention to the bird. Birds quickly learn that this noisemaking is an excellent way to get some attention. It is crucial that you do not let a bird manipulate you by screaming from the beginning of your relationship. If the screaming behavior is well established it will take time and patience to eradicate. If the behavior has not been fully mastered, a bit of management can keep it from turning into a serious dilemma.

In fact, whenever your bird is screaming it is probably a good idea to ignore it, with the following exceptions:

The Tantrum and the Squirt Bottle

I am sometimes criticized for advocating the use of spray bottles on a bird that is screaming. I'd like to clarify why and when I think a squirt bottle is an excellent way to interrupt a bird who is screaming.

For general discipline, I do not like to use squirt bottles (discipline usually doesn't accomplish anything), but they can be indispensable for curbing screaming that is part of a tantrum. I see this tantrum behavior most commonly in birds who have already learned that they can get their way by screaming.

A tantrum usually involves the whole body with the bird sort of hopping up and down and the scream is the bird's demand to get its way RIGHT NOW!!! It is important to interrupt the tantrum and create an undesirable result to this out of control behavior. For this I think a quick squirt is ideal. Aim for the body, not the head, and use only a few squirts and then ignore the bird. If it doesn't work right away, try something else. You are not trying to hurt the bird, just to interrupt the tantrum and startle it slightly.

Do not pay attention to a screaming bird. If your bird screams for attention every day when you come home, it is a good idea to wait until the bird has quieted down for a few minutes before you take it out to play. Whatever you do, don't succumb to temptation and yell, "Be quiet!" at the bird, it may think you want to make a contest out of it.

The Sentry

In the wild birds scream loudly to warn the flock (now your family) of potential threats. Can your bird see out a window. Perhaps it sees a hawk, owl, dog, mailman or some other thing that it feels it must warn you about. If your bird is frequently, letting out shrill alarm screams, it is best for your birds sense of security to move the cage away from the view.

The Crying Bird

Some birds, particularly those that have become over-dependent on their human companions, are not very adept at switching from being out of the cage with people to being by themselves. The screams you will hear after they are returned to their cage are plaintive and sorrowful sounding. I have discovered that birds with this over-dependence problem need some help with the transition from being in company to being alone. Spending a little extra time putting these birds back in their cage settling them down into being alone in somewhat the same way you would tuck a child into bed, helps them learn to adjust. I also find it helpful for these birds to be given some favorite treat or toy when they are put back in their cages to help distract their attention during the transition to being by themselves.

This type of screaming will often disappear when a bird feels secure in your relationship and is given a relatively stable pattern of attention.

TRICK
TRAINING

Trick Training

Tricks fall into two categories. The first is learned behavior where the bird performs an acquired behavior like riding a bicycle on cue. The second type is referred to as innovative behavior. An innovative behavior is one that your bird does naturally that amuses you. There is a description of how to do this on page 112.

Trick training, will turn into play time once your parrot learns the ropes. You will generally use the same bridge and reward for each trick. This first section contains beginning behaviors that you can teach your parrot. Master at least two beginning tricks before going on to the intermediate ones. Once your parrot has learned that it can earn a treat, get attention, and make you happy with it, their attention span and ability to learn tricks will improve.

How to tell if your bird is getting bored:

- Not interested in the reward
- Dropping the reward
- Reluctant or unwilling to perform learned behaviors
- Nervous or aggressive behavior such as beak wiping or snapping

If any of these things occur, get your bird to do one more simple behavior, bridge, reward and end the session, praising the bird. Abusing your bird's attention span will make it antagonistic towards training sessions.

If your bird becomes antagonistic to the training sessions, there are a few things you can try:

- Change the training treat
- Have a friend observe the training session to see if your gestures or tone of voice are frightening the bird
- Change the training time
- Shorten the training sessions
- Slow down, go back to an earlier step in the trick or try simpler behaviors
- Remove all food bowls from the bird's cage for 1-2 hours before the training session (a hungry bird is more attentive)

Note: I do not recommend the "starvation" methods endorsed by many respected trainers. A common recommendation is to allow free-feeding for only one hour per day. It does assure a dependable, attentive bird, but I think this method is both inhumane and unnecessary.

Behaviors will take varying times to learn, depending on the rapport between the trainer and the bird.

If the bird gets nervous or frightened, slow down and calm the bird. Sitting on the floor with the bird can be an excellent method.

Decide on your cues, bridges, rewards, and punishments before beginning a session.

Remember the three elements to successful communication with your bird;

1. Be Consistent

2. Be Consistent

3. Be Consistent

BEGINNING TRICKS

Begin trick training with one or more of the tricks in this section. These tricks are easy, straightforward and will allow your bird to develop trust, attention span and an understanding of cues, bridges and rewards.

Wave Hello

Needs: T-Stand
      Reward
      Cue and Bridge

 Lesson Time: 5-15 minutes depending on the bird's attention span

Description: The wave is a behavior in which the bird stands on one foot while waving up and down with the other, as if waving hello. This behavior is quickly learned, but you must be very quick with your bridge.

1   With your bird quietly perched on a T-stand, reach out your hand as if you want your bird to step onto it.

2   As soon as your bird lifts its foot, bridge and reward it. Do not allow the bird to get onto your hand.

3   Repeat step 2, this time using a cue while offering your hand. As soon as your bird lifts its foot, bridge and reward it. While repeating the cue, gradually begin to move your hand farther away from the bird until it cannot reach your hand. Your bird will begin to realize that you are rewarding it for picking up its foot.

4   With your hand back, give your cue while moving your hand up and down. The bird should try to follow your motion. Bridge and reward the bird when you see it begin to follow your up and down motion in addition to picking up its foot.

5 With your hand 5-8 inches away from the bird, wave while giving the cue. Delay the bridge and reward until the bird is mimicking the up and down motion fully.

6 With your hand further away (perhaps a foot), begin to decrease your waving motion to a finger waggle as you deliver the cue.

NOTE: For professional birds, you can slowly eliminate the verbal command. The finger waggle alone is an easily hidden cue mechanism. In case your bird begins to incorporate its behavior with its cue, use "Hi," "Hello," "Hi There," or something similar. If your bird says a lot of Hello variations, use only a hand cue. The reason for this is so that the bird is not getting cued by people who know its vocabulary, without also being bridged and rewarded.

Give a Kiss

Needs: Reward
      Cue and Bridge

 Lesson Time: 5-15 minutes

This is my favorite behavior to teach a bird. It's simple, fun and can be taught with the bird perching on your hand.

1 Place a treat between your teeth and another in your hand where the bird can see them. Direct the bird to your mouth with the treat in your hand. Let the bird take the treat from between your teeth, bridge and reward with the treat in your hand.

2 Repeat step 1, gradually eliminating the hand signal. The bird will begin to go for the treat in your lips after a few rounds as a response to the cue.

3 When the bird is moving toward your mouth on its own, cover the treat with your lips as the bird's beak makes contact. Bridge and reward the bird with the treat in your hand as soon as its beak contacts your lips. Don't allow the bird to take the treat from between your teeth.

4 Repeat step 3 several times. Next, eliminate the treat between your teeth. Direct the bird toward your lips with the treat in your hand while cueing. As the bird's beak contacts your lip, bridge and reward. Gradually decrease the motion of your hand until the bird is responding to the verbal or subtle hand cue.

Note: Do not reward the bird if it bites or pinches your lip, it should simply touch your lips with its beak.

Nod Yes

Needs: T-Stand
Reward
Cue and Bridge

 Lesson Time: 5-15 minutes depending on the birds attention span

Description: Nodding Yes is another simple behavior you can teach your parrot to perform.

1 With the bird quietly perched, hold a treat between your fingers, just out of the bird's reach. Once the bird notices the treat, move your hand up and down while giving the cue for Nod Yes. As the bird begins to follow your hand motion with its head, bridge and reward.

2 Gradually moving your hand farther away from the bird, repeat the cue. As the bird moves its head up and down, bridge and reward. As your hand moves farther away from the bird, it will begin to realize it is being rewarded for its nodding behavior.

3 Decrease the movement of your hand each time you repeat the trick, while giving the cue. You will eventually eliminate the hand cue altogether. At first, you will be rewarding the bird for any up or down motion of its head. Gradually increase your expectations until the bird bobs its head several times before being bridged and rewarded.

Note: Using a hand cue for this behavior means that you can use it in a show—occasionally asking the parrot questions and having it nod its head yes (or No—see next trick). Because the Nod Yes/Nod No/Wave Hello behaviors are very similar, cues for each behavior should be clearly distinct from one another.

Nod No

Needs: T-Stand
Rewards
Cue and Bridge

 Lesson Time: 5-15 minutes depending on the bird's attention span

Description: *Nodding No is another simple behavior to get your parrot to perform, but it can be a little confusing to some parrots who have just mastered yes. Be sure that your verbal cues for Yes/No sound different. This trick is virtually the same as Nod Yes.*

1 With the bird quietly perched hold a treat between your fingers, just out of the bird's reach. Once the bird notices the treat, move your hand from side to side while giving the cue for Nod No. As the bird begins to follow your hand motion with its head, bridge and reward it.

2 Gradually moving your hand farther away from the bird, repeat the cue. As your hand moves farther away from the bird it will begin to realize it is being rewarded for its behavior.

3 Decrease the movement of your hand while giving the cue, gradually eliminating the hand movement altogether. At first, you will reward the bird for any side to side motion of its head. Gradually, you will increase your expectations, until the bird shakes its head several times before being bridged and rewarded.

Note: You can also teach this trick by placing a piece of tape on the bird's head. Be sure that the stickiness of the tape is not excessive for the bird's feathering. The bird will try to shake the tape off, bridge and reward. Using a hand cue for this trick makes it very versatile. I like to begin a bird show with the question, "Do you know any tricks?" and have the bird vigorously nod its head No.

Parrot's Card Trick

Needs: Deck of Cards
      Cue
      Bridge and Reward

 Lesson Time: 5-15 minutes depending on the bird's attention span

Description: This card trick takes advantage of the parrot's propensity for destroying things. The only difficult part of this trick is getting the card back from the bird before it is completely destroyed.

1 Fan a deck of cards in front of the bird and use the cue, "Pick a card." When the bird takes a card, let it bite the card. Bridge and reward the bird.

2 Repeat step one until the bird quickly releases the card to get its reward. Do not wrestle the card away from the bird.

Note: This trick is great in a show. Place the disfigured card in the deck and then retrieve it, asking the parrot, "Is this your card?" To which the parrot vigorously nods No.

INTERMEDIATE
BEHAVIORS

A bird must understand the training process before progressing to the tricks in this section. Begin the tricks in this section only after your bird has mastered hand-training and two or more beginning tricks.

The Eagle

Needs: T-Stand
       Reward
       Cue and Bridge

Lesson Time: 10-15 minutes. This is an intermediate behavior. Your bird should master beginning behaviors before attempting this.

Description: This behavior is a wonderful way to show off the beauty of your bird. A bird must be comfortable in its surroundings to perform this behavior well. Be sure to train the bird to fully extend its wings to make this trick most impressive.

If the bird objects to being touched under its wings:

1 With the bird perched calmly on your hand, tilt your hand while giving the verbal cue. The bird will spread its wings to regain its balance. As soon as the bird extends its wings, bridge and reward.

2 Next, use a verbal cue just before you tilt your wrist. As you tilt your wrist and the bird lifts its wings, bridge and reward. Repeat 5-10 times.

3 As you cue the bird, gradually decrease the tilt of your hand until it is completely eliminated. The bird will eventually lift and spread its wings in response to the cue alone.

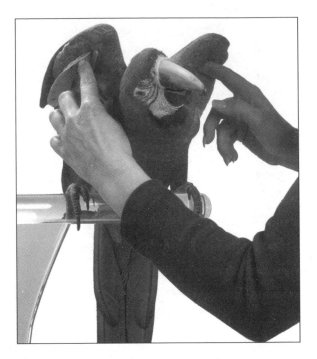

If the bird enjoys being touched under its wings:

1 With the bird on a perch, use your index fingers to gently scratch beneath its wings. Use your fingers to gently spread the bird's wings outward. As the bird lifts and stretches its wings, bridge and reward.

2 Next, use a verbal cue just before you gently stroke the underside of the bird's wings. As the bird lifts its wings, bridge and reward. Repeat this step until the bird responds reliably, fully lifting and extending its wings.

---

3 Gradually eliminate the use of your fingers, graduating to a verbal cue or hand signal. The bird should learn to lift and spread its wings when it is cued.

Note: Using both a verbal and a hand cue allows you to gradually eliminate one of them, as you decide which is easier for you to use.

Shake Hands

Needs: T-Stand
      Reward
      Cue and Bridge

Lesson Time: Because it can confuse a newly hand tamed bird, this is an intermediate behavior. Wait until the bird is familiar with the training process before attempting this behavior. You can spend 10-20 minutes per session working on this behavior.

Description: Shaking hands is a behavior somewhat like waving hello. The bird stands on one foot while lightly grasping one of your fingers and moving it up and down, as if shaking hands. This behavior is usually quickly learned, but do not allow the bird to get onto your hand. The cue for this behavior must be very different from the one you use to get the bird onto your hand.

---

1 With your bird quietly perched, reach out your hand as if you want your bird to step onto it. Allow the bird to grasp one finger and begin shaking in a gentle up and down motion, bridge and reward. (Do not let the bird get up onto your hand).

2 As soon as your bird replaces its foot on the T-stand, give the cue while offering your finger. Do not allow the bird to get onto your hand. Repeat the shaking gesture, bridge and reward. If you want to use a hand cue, begin to incorporate it with the trick at this stage. Birds have excellent eyesight and you can make the cue wiggling a single finger. A bird can differentiate this motion from that of being offered the side of your hand for perching.

3 Repeat step two 5-10 times and then cue the bird without offering your finger. The bird should pick up its foot and initiate the handshake. Bridge and reward. At this stage you can gradually eliminate the verbal cue if you desire.

Lights Out

Needs: Wall-mounted light switch
   Reward
   Cue and Bridge

 Lesson Time: 10-20 minutes.

Description: In this behavior, the bird turns off the lights from a wall mounted switch. Many birds will discover this trick if their cage is close enough to a wall switch. But beware, if given enough time, a large parrot can chew through the insulation on the switch and electrocute itself.

---

1 With the bird perched calmly on your hand, place it in front of the wall switch. In time the bird will grab the switch in its beak, bridge and reward.

---

2 Next, with the bird in front of the switch, use the cue you've chosen for Lights Out, and as the bird grabs the switch, bridge and reward.

3
With the bird watching, flip the switch on and off a few times. Once more, place the bird within reach of the switch and give the cue. As the bird grabs the switch, gently assist the bird in pulling it down by placing one finger on top of its beak and applying pressure. As soon as the light goes off, bridge and reward the bird.

4
Repeat step three 4-6 times, assisting the bird with moving the light switch. Gradually allow the bird to perform the behavior without help from you.

Note: This trick can be a fun (and effective) way to get the kids off to bed!

Banker Parrot

Needs: A table where the bird can move around
      Rewards
      Clean Quarters or Half Dollars
      Bowl and Piggybank
      Cue and Bridge

Lesson Time: 10-20 minutes. This is an intermediate behavior. Your bird should have mastered beginning behaviors and understand the bridge and reward before attempting this.

Description: This behavior has a few steps to it, and it takes a little patience to weave the various required behaviors together. Birds love to place objects inside of other objects, and every bird I have tried this with has figured out the game. Most birds love this trick and will play this game on their own if given the props.

1 Prepare a table top with a few clean, large-sized coins (not small coins that can be swallowed), and a cup or a bowl. Place your bird on the table and wait for him to pick up a coin and place it in the bowl, bridge and reward. You'll hear a loud noise when the coin drops so it isn't necessary to watch the bird closely.

2 Remove the coins from the table. Offer the bird a coin from your hand, and give the cue. When the bird drops the coin in the bowl, bridge and reward. Repeat step 2 until the bird quickly takes its cue.

3 Now, with the piggybank in front of the bird, drop a coin into the slot. Give a coin to the bird and cue. The bird will probably have a little difficulty with the slot at first, but with some practice, the bird will become adept at filling the bank.

Basketball

Needs: Table
      Bird Basketball Set
      Reward
      Cue and Bridge

Lesson Time: 10-20 minutes. This is an intermediate behavior. Your bird should master beginning behaviors before you attempt this one.

Description: In this behavior, the bird picks up a specially designed basketball and lands it through a hoop. You can find a suitable ball at a toy store. It needs to have openings that the bird can grasp with its beak, a wiffle ball will work great. This trick can be taught in much the same way as the banking trick. NOTE: Two birds who get along well can be very entertaining "playing basketball" together. This is a terrific way to entertain visiting children.

1 Prepare a large tabletop with a ball and basket. Place the bird on the table with the ball in front of it. As the bird picks up the ball, bridge and reward.

2 Use the treat in your hand to direct the bird to the basket. As the bird approaches the basket, use the treat in your hand to direct the bird to place the ball in the basket. When the bird does place the ball in the basket, bridge and reward.

3 Next, hand the ball to the bird while giving the cue. Gradually decrease the direction that you give with the treat in your hand. When the bird drops the ball in the basket, bridge and reward.

4 Repeat step two until the bird is quickly taking the ball to the basket without being directed with its treat. Bridge and reward at the moment the bird releases the ball into the basket.

Note: Since birds are imitative you can speed up the learning process by setting an example. Before beginning the training session play with the basketball set, making baskets, while the bird is watching. See page 129 for where to purchase Bird Basketball sets.

Fetch

Needs: A Small Durable Bird Toy
       Reward
       Cue and Bridge

Lesson Time: 10-20 minutes. This is an intermediate behavior. Your bird should master a few beginning behaviors before attempting this.

Description: In this behavior, the bird learns to chase after something you throw, and bring it back to you. This can be a great way to make sure your parrot gets plenty of exercise, and can be used in many ways to build a show. This behavior must be taught in several steps. First, the bird must learn to drop something out of its beak on cue. Second, it must learn to chase something you throw. And third, it must learn to return to you with the object.

1 With the bird on a table, place the object you will use for this trick in front of the bird. Let the bird play with the object. When the bird releases the object from its mouth, bridge and reward. Repeat 4-5 times.

2 The next time the bird picks up the object, give the cue to release. When the bird drops the object, bridge and reward. Repeat this step 5-10 times.

3 Show this same object to the bird and toss it a short distance. When the bird gets the object in its beak, use the cue for release. As the bird releases the object from its beak, bridge and reward. Repeat this step 5-10 times.

4 Throw the object, using the cue for Fetch. Gradually increase the distance the bird travels toward you before you bridge and reward. The bird will naturally return to you for its treat. Do not reward the bird for dropping the object and running back to you. At first, meet the bird half way, but then gradually increase your expectations until the bird is coming all the way back and dropping the object in front of you.

ADVANCED BEHAVIORS

The behaviors in this section require a high level of trust and communication between bird and trainer, as well as an understanding by your bird of the training process. Do not attempt these tricks before mastering at least two intermediate behaviors.

By this time you are becoming an accomplished trainer and you will begin to notice subtle differences in the level of communication you share with your bird. Allow what you know to enter your training session!

Riding Toys

Needs: Smooth Floor Surface
   Bird Skates, Bicycle, or other Riding Toy
   Reward
   Cue and Bridge

Lesson Time: 15-20 minutes. This is an
advanced behavior requiring a level of trust
between bird and trainer.

*Description: Birds on bicycles, scooters and roller skates
are a big hit with audiences. This behavior requires a bird
with an adventurous personality. It should only be
attempted with a bird that seems comfortable and eager
to play with the riding toy.*

1	With your bird on a smooth surface, coax it onto the riding toy from your hand. Be careful not to rush the bird. When the bird is on the toy, bridge and reward.
2	Allow the bird to get a grip with both feet and balance itself. When the bird is balanced, help the bird to move forward; bridge and reward.
3	Repeat steps one and two 5-10 times, adding the cue. Gradually decrease the amount of help you give the bird getting onto the toy. Bridge and reward the bird for getting on the toy unaided.
4	Next, allow the bird to begin moving the toy forward on its own. At first, reward the bird for any forward momentum. Gradually increase your expectations by withholding the bridge and reward until the bird has ridden several feet on its own.

Note: See page 129 for where to purchase riding toys.

Talking On Cue

Needs: T-Stand
      Reward
      Cue and Bridge

Lesson Time: 15-20 minutes. This is an advanced behavior which requires that your bird understands the training process.

Description: Many, but not all, birds can be taught to talk on cue. Observe when your talking bird is most talkative and schedule your training sessions then. Do not reward a word that you did not cue. The bird will begin to repeat words or a single word incessantly, simply to get a treat.

1 During your bird's talkative time of day, place it on a perch in front of you. Let the bird see its treats and then give it a cue. Using the word you want repeated while also giving a hand cue is the simplest first lesson. When you get the desired response, bridge and reward.

2 Repeat the process until the bird has firmly established that it is being rewarded for the proper response. When the bird is responding immediately with the desired word or phrase, move on to a new word or phrase.

3 When teaching a new word or phrase, two things must be done. First, ensure that all of the cues are clearly different from one another to avoid confusion. Second, reinforce the learned words or phrases by having the bird perform each one it knows at least once every other training session.

Questions & Answers

Needs: T-Stand
     An Assistant
     Reward
     Cue and Bridge

🕐 **Lesson Time: 15-20 minutes. This is an advanced behavior which requires that your bird understands the training process.**

Description: Question & Answer training can be difficult, but it is highly rewarding. In this session, an assistant will be answering you in the way that you want the bird to answer you (acting as a model for the behavior). Your bird must be familiar with the cue-bridge-reward sequence in order to learn this behavior quickly.

---

1 During your bird's talkative time of day, place it on a perch in front of you with an assistant standing beside the bird and facing you. Give a cue in the form of a question (e.g., "How are you?") and have your assistant give the proper reply (e.g., "I'm fine"); bridge and reward *your assistant*. You may want to include a hand signal along with the verbal cue.

2 Repeat step one. Direct your attention and eye contact to the bird but have your assistant keep responding. When your assistant responds, direct your attention to the assistant and ignore the bird.

3 After about ten rounds with the assistant, try working with the bird alone. When the bird gives the proper reply, bridge and reward. Reinforce the behavior at least four times before ending the session. If possible, hold another training session later in the day. Never reward the bird for the wrong response.

Note: With patience, this type of training can be done without an assistant. You simply cue and wait for the desired response. Try structuring a cue around one of your bird's favorite words or phrases. See more suggestions for speech training on pages 23 through 34.

Whispering Parrot

Needs: T-Stand
   Rewards
   Cue and Bridge

Lesson Time: This trick is great for any bird whether it talks clearly or not. You can spend 10-20 minutes per session working on this trick.

Description: The whisper is an adorable behavior to teach a bird and can be used in many ways in a show. Take care to have the bird's beak just touching your ear (not pinching or biting), and mumbling softly. The trick has two steps. First the bird learns to make low whispering noises on cue, and then it learns to lean into your ear while doing so.

1 During a time in the day when your bird is talking softly or muttering to itself, bridge and reward it for its behavior. The consistency of the noise is not important, the noise level is.

2 Begin to use a verbal cue until the bird mutters or mumbles something, bridge and reward.

3 When the bird quickly responds to the verbal cue by muttering, show the bird the treat in your hand. Direct it toward your ear with the treat while you cue the muttering behavior. It is not necessary to have the bird contact your ear—leaning into your ear works great. Once the bird mutters while leaning into your ear, bridge and reward.

4 Decrease the amount of direction you give the bird with your hand, and gradually eliminate the verbal cue. Your final goal is to have the bird lean toward your ear and mutter, as a response to your subtle hand cue.

Natural Behaviors

Needs: T-Stand
       Reward
       Bridge and Cue

Lesson Time: 15-20 minutes. This is an advanced behavior which requires that your bird understands the training process.

Description: This is the way to condition any behavior that your bird already performs on its own, on cue. As you are watching your bird play, think of how you can incorporate its natural behaviors into unique tricks. This training session will begin with your bird playing in its own environment, preferably an open playground. I'll use stretching as the sample behavior.

---

1 As you observe the bird standing on one foot stretching its wing and leg, bridge and reward it. It will normally stretch the opposite side. Cue the bird just before you see it shifting its weight. As the bird goes into a stretch, bridge and reward. Repeat this step the next few times you see your bird stretching.

2 Use a distinct cue that the bird will clearly recognize as different from any of its other cues. Be patient, repeating the cue, mimicking the desired behavior if necessary. Bridge and reward the parrot as soon as it performs the behavior.

Reinforcement is crucial to conditioning natural behaviors. Have your bird perform these behaviors several times in each training session. You can have an impromptu two-minute training session with your bird a few times a day.

3 Natural behaviors can be incorporated into many performance routines. The above stretch can be incorporated into a magic show where the parrot gets to be the assistant sitting on the magician's shoulder. The cue is, "And my distinguished assistant 'Paco!'"

Note: Include a lot of conditioned, natural behaviors to formulate your parrot's own, unique routine. This is the easiest way to create a distinctive, exciting, and perhaps educational show.

Table Manners

Needs: Spoon
       Honey
       Bird's favorite treat
       Cue and Bridge

Lesson Time: This is a less structured trick. Don't worry about your bird's attention span here.

Description: This is a fun way to interact with your parrot and an adorable behavior to show off casually to friends. This is a trick your parrot may figure out for itself.

1 Use honey to adhere a small piece of the parrot's favorite food to a spoon. Encourage the bird take the spoon handle in its claw.

2 Wait until the bird lifts the spoon to its beak and use your bridging word or sound just before the bird "rewards" itself.

3 If the parrot doesn't initiate the behavior with the food in its bowl, apply more honey and dip the spoon in its feed dish. Make sure that the spoon isn't too heavy for the bird to manipulate. Once the bird grasps the spoon from its bowl repeat step two.

4 Once the bird is picking up the spoon easily, begin using a cue word before offering the bird the spoon. Quite a few birds I have known have learned the cue word and use it liberally as a request for treats!

Note: Do not allow your bird to eat at the table at meal times unless you are prepared to always let it join you. The ruckus created by a bird deprived of its dinner time with the family will ruin any dinner party! I've met many bird owners who have learned this lesson the hard way.

Acrobatic Parrot

Needs: T-stand (or can be taught from the hand)
      Bridge
      Cue and Reward

Lesson Time: 5-10 minutes. This is an advanced behavior which requires trust from your bird.

Description: In this trick the bird hangs upside down on cue. Most birds love to do this as long as they have trust in their handler. Some birds will hang from one leg. I say, "Ta Da!" in the hope that a parrot will mimic me. Some do.

1 With the parrot perched on your hand (on the T-stand is O.K.), show it the reward. Bring the hand with the reward in it down below the hand the parrot is perched on. As the bird reaches for the treat, move it further and further away, until the bird is upside down, bridge and reward. Repeat this step 5-10 times

2 Next, using the cue first, repeat step one. Again, when the bird is hanging upside down, bridge and reward. Repeat this step 5-10 times.

3 Gradually eliminate using the treat to get the parrot upside down. This can be done by hiding the treat from the bird while moving your hand in the same motion, and then by gradually decreasing the motion of your arm to nothing. Your final cue can be either verbal or a discreet finger waggle.

Play Dead

Needs: Bridge
      Cue
      Reward

Lesson Time: 5-10 minutes. This is an advanced behavior which requires a great deal of trust from your bird.

Description: In this behavior, the bird will lie on its back at your command. Your bird must first become comfortable with lying on its back. Choose a time when things are quiet and the bird is in a trusting mood.

1 Sit down with the bird perched on your hand and gently turn it on its back. The simplest way to get a bird to lay on its back is to gently hold the bird against your chest and lean forward, using the hand the bird is not perched on as a cradle for its back and wings. Even the gentlest bird will probably grab your hand with its beak in an attempt to right itself. Reassure the bird until you can get it to lie somewhat still in your hand, bridge the bird, turn it gently upright and reward it.

2 Using the cue, turn the bird over onto its back. As the bird lies still for a moment, bridge, turn upright, and reward. Repeat step 2 several times.

3 When the bird is lying on its back, gently remove the bird's feet from the hand it was perched on. When the bird lies still for a few counts, bridge the bird, turn it upright, and reward. Repeat step 3 several times.

Note: The hardest part of this behavior is to get the bird to release its feet from the hand it was perched on. Cupping your free hand, gently cover the bird's head, then lift and tilt the hand the bird is perched on. In essence you are "dumping" the bird into your free hand. When the bird is upside down, wiggle your hand out of its clutches. As soon as the bird releases your hand, bridge, wait four counts, turn the bird upright, and reward. The final goal is to have the bird obediently accept being turned upside down, releasing its grip on your hand without a struggle, and laying still for a few beats.

Getting Work for Your Bird

Depending on where you live, you can make your trained pet available to film makers, ad agencies, or as entertainment at special events. If you live near a major metropolitan area, call a local talent agency and ask if they will represent a trained bird.

Performing animals must be reliable.

If you have no luck finding an agent, there will probably be a nearby film-makers' resource agency listed in the yellow pages. Ask your local reference librarian for help in tracking it down.

Requirements

Performing animals must be in top physical condition—no feather plucking or chewed tail feathers. When clipping your bird's wings, leave the two outermost primary feathers intact. This will create a smoother line, while still keeping your bird safe.

Performing animals must be reliable. Imagine showing up for the filming of a commercial, where it is costing the advertisers thousands of dollars per hour to shoot, and finding that your bird is reluctant to perform under the lights. Take a few test runs in a busy area before accepting any paid assignments.

The rate you can charge for a performing animal varies greatly depending on where you live and the medium in which the animal will be used. A steadily performing animal can make a healthy income by anyone's standards, especially if it is used repeatedly for television commercials.

If your bird is an exceptional performer, I recommend pursuing a talent agent. If there is not a talent agent in your area who is willing to handle animals, send information on your pet to local advertising agencies—to the attention of the Creative Director. The Creative Director oversees the creation of ad campaigns, and your pet may give him some inspiration. If you can afford it, use video tape. If not, at least include a photo and a detailed description of your pet's unique qualities and behavior.

If you would like to provide entertainment for fairs, special events and children's parties, contact local caterers and party planners. Arrange to show them your bird's act, set an agreeable hourly rate, and tell them how to contact you. Most party planners will charge more to their clients than they pay you, and that's standard. If you want to find your own clients, put an ad in local newspapers and the yellow pages.

Sample Pet Resume

LUCIANO PARROTTI
Species: African Gray

Special Qualities:

This bird has an exceptional speaking voice and quickly learns new phrases. He will perform simple behaviors such as nodding his head, waving, bowing, and playing dead. Has performed reliably in public and on camera numerous times. New behaviors may be trained on request with two weeks advance notice.

What to Include

For this bird I would include a black and white glossy photograph, taken at a professional portrait studio (they'll get a real kick out of it!), and an audio cassette that is humorously narrated and demonstrates the bird's speaking voice. Just remember, trick-trained birds are amusing. Make your bird's promotional package the highlight of somebody's day.

Putting a Show Together

Your bird's personality and talents will dictate how you will structure a bird show. A talking bird is a fascinating animal and this ability should always be highlighted in a show. A beautiful bird is wonderful to see and touch. If your bird is a colorful one, make sure to teach it The Eagle so that you can show off its plumage. Even in a rural area where you may not get any high-paying commercial work, you can earn money entertaining children at birthday parties or fairs.

Putting together a show with a trained bird is the best part of behavior conditioning and trick training. I encourage you to condition your bird to perform any of its unique behaviors on cue and incorporate these into your show.

Below is a script for a show featuring a talking bird who knows Nod Yes, Nod No, The Eagle, Give a Kiss, Acrobatic Parrot, Sleepy Parrot/Play Dead, Bowing (a natural behavior) and Talking on Cue.

Handler: Hi, my name's Jennifer and this is "Mr. Wonderful".

The bird, perched on the handler's shoulder, extends one wing and foot, as if bowing, and says, "Ta Da!" The handler removes the bird from her shoulder and places it on a T-stand.

Handler: Well Mr. Wonderful, do you want to do some tricks for these people?

Mr. Wonderful vigorously Nods No.

Handler: Well, would you like some treats?

Mr. Wonderful vigorously Nods Yes.

Handler: O.K. then, would you just tell everyone what kind of bird you are.

Mr. Wonderful performs The Eagle declaring, "I'm an Eagle!"

Handler picks up Mr. Wonderful and says, "Someone must have fed you goof loops! You're not an Eagle."

Mr. Wonderful hangs upside down from the handler's hand and says, "I feel fine."

Upright on the handler's hand, Mr. Wonderful performs sleepy parrot.

Handler: Well, I'm afraid Mr. Wonderful is too tired to go on.

Mr. Wonderful gets up and performs Whispering Parrot.

Handler: Oh, Mr. Wonderful says it's Sarah's 5th birthday, and he wants to give her a birthday kiss.

When the child gets up, show the child how to properly hold the bird and how to cue the bird to give a kiss. The handler will immediately take the bird back; bridge and reward.

End of show.

> Notes: You'll notice that this show is not very long. A single parrot will not perform for any extended period of time (more than 10 minutes) without becoming soured to performing. Most bird shows feature several birds who each perform for less than 5 minutes. You can stretch the show by introducing your bird and giving some background on its exceptional qualities. If you are looking toward Movies or TV you will want to train several identical birds the same behaviors.

To prepare for the "big time" ask friends and relatives to act as an audience while you "dress rehearse" your parrot. If you can't get a ready audience, go to a park or shopping center and put your bird through its paces. Parrots need time to adjust to new places, sights and sounds and it's a good idea to take a performing bird out in public as much as possible during the training phase You'll probably draw a crowd!

Afterword

I hope this book has been enjoyable and understandable for you.

If you are training your bird to be a star I hope you'll remember me on David Letterman's show. If you are training your bird to channel its energy and to build a closer relationship (as I do), I know you'll be pleased with the results of your efforts.

Your bird has amazing potential, and I hope I have helped you uncover some of the reasons why it does what it does. You needn't be an exceptional animal handler to succeed. If you can be patient, creative, and know how to set rules that both you and your birds can live with, then you are on your way!

Bon Voyage.

You can order bird training props from our retail division:

Pet Bird Xpress
42307 Osgood Rd-Unit N
Fremont CA 94539
800-729-7734

Suppliers of t-stands and props for bird taming and training.

Cast of Characters

HARLEQUIN MACAW
"Elmo"

GOFFIN COCKATOO
"Miss Thing"

AFRICAN GREY
"Sassy"

MILITARY MACAW
"Gua"

DOUBLE YELLOW-HEADED AMAZON
"Boomer"

UMBRELLA COCKATOO
"Flaxie"

BLUE FRONT AMAZONS
"Bucko" *and* **"Jorah"**

ECLECTUS
"Forrest Gump"

Did you Borrow This Book?

If you would like to order additional copies, please contact:

Parrot Press/Pet Bird Xpress
42307 Osgood Rd-Unit N
Fremont CA 94539
Phone 510-659-1030
TOLL FREE 800-729-7734
Fax: 510-659-1336

All Major Credit Cards Accepted

Single copies are $14.95 plus $3 Shipping and Handling. If you are ordering within California please add state sales tax.

Trade Inquiries Welcome